Just Do It!

Thirty Day Devotional & Inspirations for Prayer

by

Ira J. Acree

Just Do It: Thirty Day Devotional & Inspirations for Prayer
By: Ira J. Acree, Copyright © 2018

ISBN 13: 978-1-947288-44-7
IBSN 10: 1-947288-44-x

All rights reserved solely by the author. Except where designated, the author certifies that all contents are original and do not infringe upon the legal rights of any other person or work. No part of this book may be reproduced in any form without the permission of the publisher.

All Scripture quotations are taken from the following versions of the Holy Bible, New International Version®, **NIV**®. Copyright © 1973, 1978, 1984, 2011 by Biblica, Inc.™ Used by permission of Zondervan. All rights reserved worldwide. www.zondervan.com. The King James Version of the Bible and the New King James Version®. Copyright © 1982 by Thomas Nelson, Inc. Used by permission. All rights reserved.

Printed in the United States
10 9 8 7 6 5 4 3 2 1

Cover design by: Legacy Design Inc
                   Legacydesigninc@gmail.com

Published by:
Life To Legacy, LLC
20650 S. Cicero Ave, #1239
Matteson, IL 60443
(877) 267-7477
www.Life2Legacy.com

PRESENTED TO:

Contact the author at:
info@gsjbchurch.org

Dedication

It's ironic that the subtitle of this book is a "Thirty Day Devotional" because earlier this year my wife Margaret and I celebrated 30 years of marriage. For more than 30 years this beautiful woman has been walking by my side, supporting the mission that God has empowered us with, and has been praying profusely as my own personal intercessor. She has been with me through the good bad and the ugly. She has had my back through thick and thin. When I faced a serious health bout in 2016, she reached within herself and by the grace of God; she was able to aid, serve, and love me back to life.

I also dedicate this book to the entire membership of Greater St. John Bible Church. For more than 29 years, I have served this congregation. It has been a journey of a lifetime. Many lives have been changed and our community has been impacted exponentially. I have been able to serve as a pastor and as a civil rights leader in this generation with a level of success because of my wife's prayers and partnership, and because of the church's support and willingness to entrust me with the responsibility of serving. Being the leader of such a great institution has afforded me the privilege and opportunity to be an independent voice for our people. The tandem of Margaret and Greater St John has allowed me to stand tall in the face of immense opposition.

Day 1

The Power of Prayer

And he spake a parable unto them to this end, that men ought always to pray, and not to faint.
Luke 18:1

Contrary to popular belief, prayer is far more than a religious discipline or mere mind over matter therapy. The God of the universe arms every believer in Christ with this exclusive privilege and spiritual resource. The bible teaches us how to pray and what to pray for. Jesus Christ himself teaches us how to pray and gives us a model prayer and a format to follow in Matthew 6: 9-14. It gives us a guide as to the sort of things we should pray about when we approach God's throne.

Knowing the potential and power that we have with prayer, it's no surprise that Luke challenges us to embrace and practice it daily. There should never be a season in our life when we are not incorporating the spiritual discipline of prayer. The greatest benefactor in prayer is the one who's committed to it. There are so many benefits in ascribing to it, but allow me the opportunity to share some that have been completely transformative in my life. No matter what's going on in your life, prayer escorts you into God's throne room to receive grace. Prayer also charges your spiritual battery which enables you to live the victorious Christian life. It's very hard to veer off into an extended period of ungodly behavior when you have a serious prayer life, because prayer brings you into a place of authentic fellowship and intimacy with God. It gives one consolation to know that God is with you and watching every move that you make. Prayer also renews you daily and gives you a peace that assures you regardless of what you're encountering or confronting, that's if it ain't alright, it will be alright.

Day 2

A Prayer of Adoration

Bless the Lord, O my soul: and all that is within me, bless
his holy name. Bless the Lord, O my soul, and
forget not all his benefits
Psalm 103:1-2

Wherein it's great to realize the importance of prayer and the power that you potentially have when you apply it, it's also invaluable to know how to pray. I personally believe that there is not a person on earth that has mastered the "how to" of praying. As you go through this devotional, please do not be intimidated because you haven't reached the plateau of being able to pray like Daniel or Apostle Paul. I want to offer to you a four-point method of praying that an old country preacher once gave me many years ago. It's called the ACTS method of praying. The ACTS prayer model uses the acronym A.C.T. S. to help you remember four key topics for your own prayers. It closely models the topics outlined in the Lord's Prayer.

This model provides that outline to help you find the words to pray and reminds you to cover these four key topics. A is for *Adoration*. Start your prayers with praise. Praise God for who he is. Worship him and acknowledge his greatness. This step is important not only to shower God with praise but to align your heart with his. Praise keeps your heart and eyes focused on God. Starting with a heart full of worship reminds you just who you're praying to and what great power he has to answer your prayers. David, the poet, and psalmist, is an expert at giving adoration: In this particular psalm, he says parenthetically that I will bless the Lord! I will celebrate the Lord! I honor and salute the Lord! I extol him and I praise him! Everybody praises someone or something whether it's a professor, a teacher, a banker, a physician, a spouse or a neighbor. With that being said, David proclaims, I've determined within myself that I'm going to praise the God of my salvation. In addition to praising him with all that I have, I'm going to bless his name.

In the Old Testament, he was called many names: Elohim, El Shaddai, Jehovah Jireh, which translates to Lord my provider! Jehovah Nissi or Lord our banner! Jehovah Shalom or Lord our peace, Jehovah Tsidkenu or Lord our righteousness! The reality is they revered God and called him by the specific name in which he manifested deliverance, rescue or assistance. Many today can't speak Hebrew, but in our English language, we acknowledge God as a doctor in a sick room, a lawyer in a courtroom, a bridge over troubled water, a heart fixer and a mind regulator! David presents an excellent argument that God is worthy of adoration and praise.

Day 3

A Prayer of Confession

*If we confess our sins, he is faithful and just to forgive us
our sins, and to cleanse us from
all unrighteousness.
I John 1:9*

The second letter in the ACTS method of prayer is 'C', which stands for *Confession*. Never proceed in praying without acknowledging your sin and transgression. Be sure to tell God you're sorry for where you've fallen short, where your actions haven't lived up to His expectations, where you haven't done something you should have. Then, sincerely ask God for his forgiveness, his divine love and help to do better next time. Let me be crystal clear, the Apostle John is not by any means suggesting that humanity needs to confess or acknowledge one's sin to anyone who would listen. Confession to other Christians is a bar much too low if your goal is to obtain forgiveness from God. It also could be very unrewarding and hurtful as well. St. John is stating that when a believer confesses his or her sins, that God is so loving and gracious that he will honor his own covenant made at Mount Calvary, and forgive them of their sin. The image that is perfectly portrayed is a loving God taking our sins and pouring them in seas of forgetfulness and posting a sign that says "No fishing." Once forgiven, don't engage in a pity party, move forward. The thing to do is to repent! If we truly believe what Christ did was enough, and that

His love never fails, it's imperative that we repent from our sins. If we followed Christ and lived in a way that never involved us turning away from our sins, then we are really proclaiming what Jesus did on the cross was not enough. He paid it all at Calvary for us. His love is never-ending. His forgiveness is for all past, present, and future sins. When we confess our sins, He is there. When we cry out to Him, He is there. When we repent, He is there.

It is the birthright of every child of God to be cleansed from all sin, to keep himself blameless from the world, and to live as never more to offend his Maker. This miracle was made possible unto us as a result of Jesus' finished work on the cross. This power manifests within us once the Holy Spirit takes residence in our hearts.

Day 4

A Prayer of Thanksgiving

Be anxious for nothing, but in everything by prayer and supplication, with thanksgiving, let your requests be made known to God; and the peace of God, which surpasses all understanding, will guard your hearts and minds through Christ Jesus.
Philippians 4:6-7

The third letter in the ACTS method of prayer is 'T', which stands for *Thanksgiving*. It's easy to say I'm grateful by uttering mere words, it's a horse of another color to say it, and it is actually your reality. Apostle Paul challenges the readers and the church at Philippi to adopt an attitude of gratitude. He insists that believers in Christ be adamant about being anxious for nothing. The truth is however, we all know that is much easier said than done. We can quote scriptures until we're blue in the face. We can sing melodious gospel songs and hymns and yet cling for dear life to our worries and anxieties. The antidote to anxiety is prayer. But not just the kind of prayers that propel us to get on our knees and cause us to recite a long laundry list of our desires and wants. We need to offer prayers of thanksgiving. There is great therapy in possessing a grateful heart.

During the remainder of this thirty day consecration I challenge you to commit to the practice of counting your blessings. Before you go to sleep at night, call to mind one or two things you can be grateful for that day. From time to time pause and think of two or three persons in your life that you can be grateful for. In addition to counting your blessings, it behooves us to be ambitious and eagerly engaged in cultivating our dreams yet by the same token, don't stumble and get stifled by allowing the process to breed discontent. Nurture your dreams, but don't by any means allow them to pull you out of the present or become too attached to the outcome.

The key is sowing your seeds of intention and accepting the knowledge that worthwhile things take time to grow and develop. In the meantime, be grateful. We spend too much time complaining about what we don't have and not enough time praising God for what we have and for all of the tragedies he allowed us to miss. Gratitude is the healthiest of all human emotions. "The more you express gratitude for what you have, the more likely you will have even more to express gratitude for…Zig Ziglar

Day 5

A Prayer of Supplication

Let us therefore come boldly unto the throne of grace, that we may obtain mercy, and find grace to help in time of need.
Hebrews 4:16

The fourth letter in the ACTS method of prayer is 'S', which stands for *Supplication*, which is the action of asking or begging for something earnestly or humbly. There are many needs today in every home, city, town, and state. So many are distressed and confused by all of what the world has to offer. We have seen problems in our country that we have not seen before. The contrary winds of racism have been fanned. The country is more polarized than it's been in several decades.

The news is full of crime and hate, which has led to all types of violence on our urban streets. In our personal lives we fight a battle that we cannot see; for it is a spiritual battle that only God can help us through. This one thing I know, God loves us and won't leave us nor forsake us, and for those who come before the throne of God boldly, can find grace and help in the time of need. I said "help is on the way, help is… on the way." I want you to understand that there are times when God's answer to your prayer might not be what you want; it is not unusual for God to not always answer anything close to what you want to hear. We must understand that we may want for things that are not expedient. However, God will answer prayer and will always be with us, he just may not give us exactly what we want. Reverend James Meeks tells a story of how he and his NBA loving son had an evening planned wherein they had planned to watch a Bulls vs. Lakers game at Rev. Meeks' house.

However, late that afternoon he asked his son to run some errands with him. Wouldn't you know it, he took him to Rush Presbyterian and John Stroger Hospitals. Rev. Meeks appeared to be making hospital calls and visiting every patient in both hospitals. As the evening grew later, his son was getting upset, because it was clear that they were not going to make it back home in time to see the game. To his surprise, his father however had purchased tickets to the actual game, and since they were already at hospitals in the medical district on the Westside, they were on time. The United Center was only a couple minutes away. God is the same kind of father. He answers our requests in multiple ways; yes, no, not now and sometimes better. In this particular instance, young Meeks received an answered prayer classified as better. He got more than he desired.

Day 6

Pray for Your Family

But if serving the LORD seems undesirable to you, then choose for yourselves this day whom you will serve, whether the gods your ancestors served beyond the Euphrates, or the gods of the Amorites, in whose land you are living. But as for me and my household, we will serve the LORD."
Joshua 24:15

Joshua challenged the people to choose who they would serve and to get about it! The same choice stands before us today! It's about time people got off the fence and made up their minds whose team they are on. Joshua set the example and laid down the gauntlet for the rest of the people by stating his clear intention to serve God. We need some more Joshua's in our day! We need some men and women who will settle it in their hearts that Jesus Christ and His Word and will are going to come before everything else in life! We need some who will set the example for others. We have too many who, by their lives, give justification for slackness in life. We need some who have a backbone of steel and who would rather die than let something come ahead of God in their lives. We don't need any more excuse makers. We need more men who will say like Stephen in the New

Testament, some things are worth dying for.

There is a need for more Joshua's, men who will embrace spiritual leadership and its many challenges. Joshua spoke up for his family. The family is the oldest institution on earth and it's the most vital, significant one. The government can give us better schools, it can reform the criminal justice system, increase economic investment, rebuild our challenged neighborhoods, but there is one thing that government can't do and that is to raise our children for us. This is something we must do on our own.

Once we embrace that assignment, we will start having much stronger and vibrant communities in a myriad of ways. One of the worse things you can do is to eliminate God out of your family's equation. If there is one thing I wish I would have done more of with my children when they were young and growing up in our house, it's pray. Don't just pray for your family, pray with them. Designate at least one day a week that your family comes together for a few moments of prayer. There are so many benefits to family prayer that time doesn't permit me to list them all.

Day 7

Pray for Your Church

As we have therefore opportunity, let us do good unto all men, especially unto them who are of the household of faith.
Galatians 6:10

From the biblical standpoint, it's necessary and very significant to be a part of a local church. A church family provides a vehicle or an entity where one can receive consistent biblical teaching, whether it's through sermons, bible class, Sunday school or through a particular teaching through special spiritual growth campaigns. The church is also the place where New Testament believers come together collectively to honor God through worship. There is a special tie that binds us together when believers identify as a group in worship and assemble regularly, whether it's through music, preaching or serving.

The church also provides a framework of accountability. At the church, there is someone to encourage you, to inspire you, to love on you, and even rebuke you when necessary. So many have found lifelong friends that they can confide in right within the parameters of the church. In an age wherein the church is under attack and dismissed and classified as irrelevant by some, it's important that we be reminded of how beneficial it is for one to be in relationship with a family of believers, who can encourage you along your faith journey and be supportive at the same time when the storms of life are raging. So I implore you from the depths of my heart to spend some of your precious time in prayer for your faith community. Create a list and begin praying for those who make up your spiritual family. Pray for the leaders for sure, but please be inclusive of those who labor in the diverse areas of service.

Day 8

Pray for your City

And seek the peace of the city whither I have caused you to be carried away captives, and pray unto the LORD for it: for in the peace thereof shall ye have peace.
Jeremiah 29:7

I personally believe that my unique gift to the world is not my vocal skills, my preaching gift nor is it a bubbly personality. I think it's my willingness to take my prophetic voice into the public square and dare as an ambassador of God, to speak truth to power. I have recently challenged local political leaders to put forth a vision for our city, in which its mission is to end the abysmal Tale of Two Cities that exist in Chicago. The prophet Elijah didn't hesitate to challenge King Ahab about his corrupt administration, and neither did Moses cower to Pharaoh. I ask you to pray for your city because according to the word of God, everyone has a right to the tree of life.

A study called *The Kids First Chicago* shows 1 in 4 African-American students in Chicago attends a failing school; 2 of 25 Latino students attend a failing school; only 2 of 100 white children attend a failing school. Additionally, nearly 40 percent of Black youth between the ages of 20–24 are neither working nor in school; the number of white youth in this category is only 7 percent. Poor and working people are finding themselves pushed out of west side and south side communities that their families have called home for generations due to gentrification. The homicides in Chicago are out of control, it's more than Los Angeles and New York combined.

It's a minefield out here and we need the people of God aware of the crisis state that we are in locally so that we will know specifically what to pray for. Pray for spiritual awakening in the Churches in Chicago. Pray against the spirit of violence that runs rampant throughout the city. Pray for the prosperity and welfare of our city. Pray for equity and fairness for all communities.

Day 9

Pray for Your Community

Fulfill ye my joy, that ye be like minded, having the same love, being of one accord, of one mind.
Philippians 2:2

In the bible days, churches were identified by their geographical location. For example, the Church at Corinth and the Church at Philippi were named after cities located in Greece. In 2014, I had the distinct honor of visiting Corinth, Greece with American theologian Dr. Klyne Snodgrass and North Park Theological Seminary. The Church of Ephesus was actually a town in Western Turkey. That old traditional format of naming churches was very helpful because one would easily be able to identify the church and its potential congregants based up knowing the name.

In 1985, when our church was established, we would have been called the Church of Austin if that same practice was being employed. The truth of the matter, however, although that's not our technical name, many people have called us that, because of our location and our body of community outreach work we've done over the years. I urge you to join us today in fervently praying for this community. Many are hurting and feel hopeless, because of economic disinvestment, family abandonment, being counted out and told that they are worthless and will never amount to anything. In the same spirit of unity that Paul envisioned from the church at Philippi, let us pray for every family within Austin. I urge everyone reading this devotional to commit to praying for their community. From there you can pray for the leadership and the local schools. Pray teachers raise up strong children who will mature into successful leaders themselves. Pray for every church, pastor, youth leader and leadership team in your community. Be sure to pray for the non-profits who are providing many much-needed services which include but are not limited to the marginalized, the youth, seniors and all families in need.

Day 10

Pray for your Future

"For I know the plans I have for you," declares the LORD, "plans to prosper you and not to harm you, plans to give you hope and a future."
Jeremiah 29:11

God has incredible plans in store for you. This is an excerpt from a letter to the exiles in Babylon. Nebuchadnezzar had sent some Israelites from Jerusalem to be held in Babylonian captivity. In essence, God's people were being held as prisoners of war, but Jeremiah delivered a message of hope, that God has a better plan than being prisoners and indentured servants. This message applies to all believers as well. You may not be in a place of prosperity now and you may think God has no plans for you, but you're wrong. The game of life is not over, and the King still has time to make another move. It's an awesome and spectacular plan to give you a good and prosperous future.

It matters not what juncture you're at in life. You may be in the embryonic state of adulthood and you're saying, "I've got my whole life ahead of me. I don't need to know what I'm going to be doing in the future." You may think you don't need to know yet, and that's your choice, but the truth of the matter is, God has a plan for your future, and with knowing more about that custom designed plan, you'll be able to make quality decisions that will get you where you need to be. It's vital that you believe God has a great future planned for you and it's also crucial that you trust him with it. Trusting him with it entails praying about it.

Dr. Tony Evans tells the story of a blind girl who was caught in a fire on the tenth floor of a building. Somehow she made her way to a window but she couldn't see. She felt the heat and smelled the smoke of the fire. Then she heard a fireman yell, "Jump, jump!" She responded "I'm scared to jump. I can't see." The fireman said, "If you don't jump you're going to die. Take the risk and jump." It's bad enough to jump from ten stories high, but to jump when you can't see where you're jumping, that's terror. In the midst of the chaos, she heard another voice, "Darling, jump, I've got you." She smiled and said, "Okay daddy, I'll jump. Jesus Christ is in a similar way, is inviting us all to jump. He knows you're afraid, but just jump. We've seen what he can do. He has a track record that's trustworthy. Although you can't see him, remember He always sees you. He can be trusted.

Day 11

Pray for your Spiritual Leadership

Then the twelve called the multitude of the disciples unto them, and said, It is not reason that we should leave the word of God, and serve tables. Wherefore, brethren, look ye out among you seven men of honest report, full of the Holy Ghost and wisdom, whom we may appoint over this business.
Acts 6:2-3

One of the greatest joys I've experienced recently while preaching was when I delivered a message entitled: I Won't Complain. This message was one of a series of sermons that I preached as I journeyed through the book of Acts. This particular lesson deals with a problem that occurred when the disciples were being accused of showing favoritism. Much grumbling and murmuring was taking place within the membership which ultimately led to the origin of this biblical office as well the appointment of the church's first seven deacons. It was very liberating to me that this sermon provided me the opportunity to express my gratitude for the servant nature of this position, and I also got a chance to testify about the great example of servants that I've been honored and privileged to co-labor with down through years. The enormous joy that I received as a result of teaching on this subject had a lot to do with the fact that this message gave me an opportunity to teach about team leadership The pastor is not the only leader in the church. The pastor, his pastoral staff and the deacon's ministry are our church's spiritual leadership team. While we must honor and respect them, we must also be sure that we pray for them as well. It is vital that believers know the distinct difference that their prayers have on the lives of leadership. Pray for the pastor, ministers' staff, deacons, and each of the ministry leaders. Completing this simple request helps your church immensely. It is the very best defense against Satan's hatred of our spiritual leaders.

Day 12

Pray for Peace

*Blessed are the peacemakers: for they shall be
called the children of God.
Matthew 5:9*

As I write this meditation today, Chicago is anxiously awaiting the verdict from the people versus Jason Van Dyke trial. Many African-Americans in our city see this as the trial of the century for black Chicago. Laquan McDonald, a black seventeen-year-old male, was gunned down by a white police officer on the south side of Chicago. The fatal shooting was captured on video, as McDonald appears to be walking away from the officer, yet the officer proceeds to unload his weapon with 16 shots into the young man's body.

The defense has been unapologetic about making the case that the officer's life was threatened and so he was in essence eliminating the threat in the manner he was trained while he was a cadet in the police academy. Tensions have been exorbitantly high. Many have decried that justice is on trial. Some even suspect that the city will go up in smoke, riot style if the officer is acquitted. The family of Laquan McDonald led by his great uncle, Pastor Marvin Hunter, called for calm and asked everyone in the event that the verdict is not what we desire, to protest in a peaceful and nonviolent manner.

My colleagues from the Leaders Network are also calling for calm, but in addition to that, we are praying for peace. We are not only praying for peace in the aftermath of the trial, but we are also praying for peace to manifest in our neighborhoods, a place that sometimes feels more like battlefields. We pray for peace throughout urban America. We pray for peace within the homes and throughout the US and abroad. Blessed are the peacemakers is a part of Jesus' Sermon on the Mount. We must emulate what Jesus preached and modeled, he actually laid down his life to make peace between God and sinners. When we carry His message of peace to others, we are the peacemakers. Those who witness and share their faith in the name of Christ are ambassadors for peace, and Jesus calls us children of God.

Day 13

But my God shall supply all your need according to his riches in glory by Christ Jesus.
Philippians 4:19

One of the greatest promises of scripture is also one of the most often repeated promises. Most of us have heard this conditional promise of the Lord. The promise is that God will meet every single one of your needs. That promise is so all-inclusive that every other promise of God fits under its umbrella! You are probably asking, and I'm glad you did, "What needs does that include? And here's the answer, every last one of them! It doesn't get any better than that, does it? In fact, did you know that one of the names by which God identifies Himself in the Old Testament is "Jehovah Jireh" which means, "I am the God who provides."

Let's take another look at Philippians 4:19, "And my God will meet all your needs according to his glorious riches in Christ Jesus." Let's take the limits off the Most High and take him at his word, everything means exactly EVERYTHING! You can shop until you are blue in the face and you will never find a better deal than that. Paul was giving the church of Philippi a very encouraging promise regarding their giving. So many people just read this scripture and failed to understand or acknowledge the context.

Paul's preaching had brought about so much opposition and caused disruptions and the Philippian believers heard about it and responded by sending him financial help to bail him out of trouble with the authorities. Their help apparently had to be sent multiple times, but they loved Paul, and stood with him in the gospel; and so, they were glad to give of themselves to help him. So actually Paul tells the believers who personally supported his ministry that investing in the kingdom of God gets you an abundance of blessings. Supporting the work of the kingdom obligates God to supply all of your needs.

And that means all your needs supplied in every area of your life. So, true prosperity covers every area of life, every commodity of life, and every element of life. This message should provide a tremendous amount of hope to the remnant of believers who give selflessly and sacrificially to support the work of the church. Your sacrifice has not gone unnoticed by the Lord. So please proceed in the future by praying more confidently regarding you and your family's needs.

Day 14

Pray for Guidance and Direction

Trust in the LORD with all your heart and do not lean on your own understanding. In all your ways acknowledge Him, and He will make your paths straight.
Proverbs 3:5-6

Following divine guidance and direction has enormous benefits. God only leads a man into the profitable paths of life. He leads him into honor, beauty, dignity, and glory, making him the envy of other men. I religiously follow a divine plan, so I enjoy the benefits it offers. There have been so many times in my life when I felt I couldn't see my way but applying and having this perspective has made a great difference.

Our endorsement and confidence in the scripture should not be mistakenly used to support the notion that this assurance is a sort of blind trust that suspends critical judgment. Rather, the student of wisdom learns to have confidence that living for God is the most reasonable thing to do. God's wisdom and word are infallible and can always be trusted and looked to for the purpose of drawing from its wisdom and its inspired writing. I've often looked at these two verses with my homiletical lens and consistently pulled out a sermon entitled, "What to do when you don't know what to do." It's always a three-point message. Trust in the Lord with all your heart is the first point, and from this a clause, you are exhorted to hold on to your faith. The next segment of this passage says "And do not lean on your own understanding. In all your ways acknowledge Him," which leads me to my second point which is to hang in there through the fight. The Periscope concludes by saying and He will make your paths straight which gives the final point of the message, hold out until the future.

Day 15

Pray for Spiritual Growth

But grow in the grace and knowledge of our Lord and Savior Jesus Christ. To Him be the glory, both now and to the day of eternity.
Amen.
II Peter 3:18

Once you are saved and understand that you are totally accepted and forgiven by God, you then proceed into another stage which is a place among the sanctified. Sanctification is the process of becoming holy. It's the ongoing perpetual process of being conformed to the image of Christ. Salvation happens instantaneously, but sanctification is a lifetime process.

God looks at us as holy and righteous the moment we place our faith in his beloved Son Jesus to save us. But aligning our hearts and minds to God comes in stages. It happens as the Holy Spirit reveals God's truth to us. No wonder Peter's words in his second epistle resonates so well with so many believers. In essence he says, I know salvation is free, and I know works are not a prerequisite to receiving it by any stretch of the imagination, but he fervently admonishes us "but grow in the grace and knowledge of our Lord and Savior Jesus Christ to Him be the glory, both now and to the day of eternity. Amen"

He sounds the alarm to the body of Christ that grace is so powerful that it should produce some fruit, spiritual growth and knowledge of the word. Don't embrace the concept of cheap grace that has no impact on your heart. Let me offer three reasons why you should pray for your growth and do all in your power to grow. 1. You are an organism and growth comes with the territory. When a baby reaches a certain age, he shows some development and growth. If your child turns five years old and he's not walking or talking and is still drinking Enfamil and Similac milk, your child has some serious medical or mental issues. 2. When you grow it benefits you in every area of your life. Applying the principles of the word of God will make you a better parent, a better spouse, a better neighbor and a better co-worker. Submitting completely to the Lord also brings abundance into your life. Isaiah 1:19 tells us If ye be willing and obedient, ye shall eat the good of the land. Finally your growth impacts the kingdom, it has an evangelistic impact. When people see you embodying true Christianity, they will know you are authentic.

Day 16

Pray for Marriages

Therefore shall a man leave his father and his mother, and shall cleave unto his wife: and they shall be one flesh.
Genesis 2:24

The time must come where we stop asking of marriage what God never designed it to be—perfect happiness, conflict-free living, butterflies and sex on the beach. Marriage is serious business, and a successful union experiences more work than play.

We must learn to appreciate what God designed marriage to provide: partnership, spiritual intimacy and the ability to pursue God together. That being said, marriage is under a severe attack, like never before. Did you know that forty percent of all marriages end in divorce? Another sad reality is that Christians are flocking to divorce court as much as the secular world according to data from Focus on the Family. If any race or ethnicity needs to pray for its marriages, it is African Americans. Many single parents have done a whale of a job raising their children by themselves, but can you imagine how much stronger we could be if our families were not so fragile and fragmented.

Currently in America, 70 percent of all black children are growing up in a single family household. Every marriage has potential walk-away moments. In fact, any relationship of depth has those moments—mine certainly has. Yours will too, trust me. Leaving may feel like a quick fix, but in the long run, it doesn't solve the problem, nor does it make your life better. If you leave, you'll simply repeat the destructive cycle over and over again, missing out on the growth that comes from enduring the hard days. I believe most marriages can be saved. It's much easier to make your marriage work than to give up on it. I remember the late Pastor James T. Ross stated after celebrating his 45th wedding anniversary to his third wife, "Had I known what I know now, I could have stayed with my first wife." He later told me that he didn't know how to forgive, but all he had to do was keep on living, a day came when he needed it. As the writer says husband and wives are one flesh, once both parties allow that to resonate, with the help of God, the marriage is well on its way to prosper and thrive.

Day 17

Pray for your Children

Train up a child in the way he should go; even when he is old he will not depart from it.
Proverbs 22:6

Start early praying for your children, don't hesitate incorporating prayer into their lives. Pray specific prayers. Don't make it a practice praying prayers of generality. Be sure to pray for your child's salvation, pray for your child's health and physical safety. Pray for your child's schooling and academic successes. Secondly, speak over your children's lives, make your prayers audible. From the very beginning of the Bible, we see the power of spoken words.

The power of words is not just evident when God uses them, but the Solomon, the wisest man that ever lived, tells us that words are powerful when we speak them. Proverbs 18:21 states this truth that the power of life and death are in the tongue. Please know that you have the power to speak blessings in every area of your child's life. Lastly, never give up on your children when they stumble or stray. No matter how much of a God-fearing person you may be, it's virtually impossible to guarantee that your child will be living for Christ the entire duration of his or her life. Nevertheless, never write them off, never dog them out, just be sure to love the hell out of them. They will eventually come around. As this verse implies, they may stray away for a season but they will never depart.

Day 18

Pray for our Elderly

Rebuke not an elder, but intreat him *as a father; and the younger men as brethren; the elder women as mothers; the younger as sisters, with all purity.*
1 Timothy 5:1-2

I Was always taught to respect the elders. Weren't you? But how many of you are really respecting the elderly people around you? What reasons do you have for not doing so?

I ask you because we've all seen many elders in society not being treated well. I've even heard of people having the audacity not to respect the elderly especially the young generation.

And that's not all; even family members sometimes fail to spend time with them, which is sad.

The Bible exhorts us that respect towards the elderly, their fortitude, wisdom, knowledge, and grace should be imbibed by us, though sadly it doesn't happen.

There might be a few exceptions as I also don't believe that growing old is a sign of becoming wiser, but we shouldn't show disrespect for seniors in any case–isn't it? If you come across an elder whom you don't know, and if he/she isn't able to prove his/her worth to you–it doesn't mean that he/she doesn't deserve your respect. One of the most disturbing things for me is, it seems that

African-American young adults are more disrespectful to their elders than other races. To borrow a phrase from Rev. Al Sharpton, "Let us make a concerted effort to water our roots like other ethnics and not piss on them." Pray for the elderly today, for we owe them a great debt indeed. So many marched so long and died too young fighting for our liberation.

Day 19

Pray for the Poor

Train up a child in the way he should go; even when he is old he will not depart from it.
Proverbs 22:6

There are nearly 150 million poor and near-poor people in the United States who are not to blame for the devastation rendered by the Great Recession. Nearly one-third of the American middle class–mostly families with children–have now fallen into poverty status.

The magnitude of the Great Recession confirms that poverty is no longer a personal calamity, it is, rather, a societal crisis. Poverty is real and as Mahatma Gandhi once said: "Poverty is the worse form of violence." It's criminal for a rich nation to allow its citizens to be hungry, homeless and void of educational opportunities. It's also unchristian for followers of Christ to be insensitive to the plight of the poor. In this instance, I'm not referring to the working poor but I'm talking about people who have nowhere to lay their heads, and they are not privileged to enjoy a decent meal and have no access to healthcare. There are a few ways you can show your sensitivity for the poor. You can be a voice for the poor. So many people have no platform or advocate to speak up for them. One can also partner with those already fighting against poverty. Championing education is a way to inspire the youth to be successful and get an education. Please be sure to incorporate prayer into the equation. Invoking divine intervention on behalf of the poor always pay enormous dividends.

Day 20

Praying for Pastors

And I will give you pastors according to mine heart, which shall feed you with knowledge and understanding."
Jeremiah 3:15

Pastoring is a challenging job. You'd be surprised at the number of pastors who are depressed, discouraged and/or considering quitting the ministry. Most pastors are generally overworked and put in a minimum of 50 hours a week according to a recent survey in Christian Post. Unless you happen to pastor a mega sized church, you will more than likely be expected to be all things for all people or you will be in the proverbial doghouse. In some settings, some pastors are expected to attend every graduation, retirement party, birthday celebration, funeral and wedding. You are expected to attend to your own sick and shut-in list as well as the extended family of the membership. In addition to performing most counseling sessions, you also bear the burden of making sure that the budget is met or otherwise all eyes will be on you if the church's bills are not paid on time and if employees are not compensated. Somehow in the midst of it all, the pastor must find hours for sermon preparation. In addition to the demand on their time, many pastors also are lonely and live in isolation. Being quite aware that the clergy are often judged by a double standard, many just choose to do life alone rather than be harshly judged for being themselves. The body of Christ universally would be stronger if believers made a concerted effort to lighten the load of the local pastor. I challenge each of you to commit to helping your pastor through this spiritual minefield.

- Teach yourself to give to and not demand from him or her.
- Be sensitive of his or her time.
- Display a spirit of encouragement around the pastor and the church family.
- Pray for your pastor.

Day 21

Pray God strengthens your Devotion

This book of the law shall not depart out of thy mouth; but thou shalt meditate therein day and night, that thou mayest observe to do according to all that is written therein: for then thou shalt make thy way prosperous, and then thou shalt have good success.
Joshua 1:8

A 30-day spiritual growth campaign is always a blessing to the church and the persons who dare to take the journey because it causes us to renew our faith and to engage in spiritual consecration. I think with each consecration; we get better in some form or fashion of our life. This particular campaign, however; is targeting strengthening and improving our prayer and devotional life. It is my prayer that you are studying daily and meditating on each scripture. The bible says faith cometh by hearing and hearing by the word of God. So I urge you to be adamant about engaging in the task. Start by reading the verse and repeating it multiple times. Focus on what you read and the message being conveyed. Take it to another level by writing it down. Writing a verse down sort of forces the mind to scrutinize the verse more than reading does. Next, you must say it. Articulating it has power. Don't stop there, then, you need to sing it. Use your own music just be sure to do it. Finally, pray the scripture.

Day 22

Pray that the Gospel goes Forth

And Jesus came and spake unto them, saying, All power is given unto me in heaven and in earth. Go ye therefore, and teach all nations, baptizing them in the name of the Father, and of the Son, and of the Holy Ghost: Teaching them to observe all things whatsoever I have commanded you: and, lo, I am with you always, even unto the end of the world.
Amen.
Matthew 28:18-20

There is a lot of crime, chaos and corruption in the world today and in their desperation people are resorting to a variety of wrong options for a resolution to the madness. Some think the answer lies within the realm of politics if we just get compassionate and visionary leaders in office. Others think that money alone could solve every crisis that we encounter. Then others naively put the complete onus on the back of the family for solving the problems of the world. Wherein every institution mentioned plays a vital role in a productive and well- functioning society, only the church has the power to bring light into dark places. The truth is the real hope for the world is the church of the living God. The church does a lot of great things in the world. Since its infancy, churches have built nice buildings, established schools, fed the hungry, clothed the naked and even has helped poor countries get clean water.

The primary purpose of the church, however; is to bring the gospel to the whole world. We can never think that doing some great deeds can be a substitute for the gospel going forth. When the gospel is shared, real transformation happens in a community, in a city, in a nation, and ultimately across the world. When people live and share Jesus's gospel, hatred and racism will begin to dissipate. There is only one thing that can bring peace into the world. It is the adoption of the gospel of Jesus Christ, rightly understood, obeyed and practiced by rulers and people alike. The truth of Jesus and His finished work on the cross is something that the world must hear. As local church communities, we can bring that truth to the people closest to us. The church was given a nonnegotiable charge in the Great Commission to take the gospel to the world, we can't just wait for the hurting to come to us.

Day 23

Pray for Boldness in Witnessing

Be it known unto you all, and to all the people of Israel, that by the name of Jesus Christ of Nazareth, whom ye crucified, whom God raised from the dead, even by him doth this man stand here before you whole. This is the stone which was set at nought of you builders, which is become the head of the corner. Neither is there salvation in any other: for there is none other name under heaven given among men, whereby we must be saved. Now when they saw the boldness of Peter and John, and perceived that they were unlearned and ignorant men, they marvelled; and they took knowledge of them, that they had been with Jesus.
Acts 4:10-13

Far too many Christians are failing miserably in the arena of soul winning! There is a story I once told about a little boy who had a mongrel dog which is a simple name for a mutt. Well, on one occasion, a man asked him what kind of dog he had. The little boy responded, "He's a police dog." The man said, "he doesn't look like a police dog to me." The little boy says "he's in the secret service!" This reminds me of the modern day church. We have a whole lot of professing Christians who obviously are in the secret service. If you think witnessing is too challenging and too complex of an assignment, you're not by yourself. If you feel like you're in over your head, you're in good company because in the book of the Acts of the Apostles it displays that Peter and John didn't have impressive credentials. They had no seminary training. They never matriculated at stellar institutions like Princeton, Fuller, or Dallas Theological Seminary; nor did they train at the Trinity Evangelical Divinity School, the parallels of that day! They never attended Catalyst conference or The Samuel Proctor's conference, yet their boldness in witnessing astonished and ultimately aggravated the Jewish Leaders. They nevertheless were zealous and became bold witnesses by leaning on the power of the Holy Spirit. Hence; in spite of their inadequacies, they still managed to give a clarion call. They themselves were confident communicators and because of that, it produced crazy courage. Whenever you tie all that together witnessing becomes second nature. Please pray that God produces in you the fire to witness that Peter and John possessed.

Day 24

Pray for Wisdom

If any of you lack wisdom, let him ask of God, that giveth to all men liberally, and upbraideth not; and it shall be given him.
James 1:5

Wisdom and knowledge are two recurring themes in the holy writ of God. They are both related but are distinctly different. Knowledge is a noun that refers to the information, understanding, and skills that you gain through education or experience. It refers to the hard facts and the data that can be available to anyone if he has the right resources. For example, you can have practical, medical or scientific knowledge. Wisdom, on the other hand refers to the ability to make sensible decisions and give good advice because of the experience and knowledge that you have.

Most of us know that you can have a lot of book sense and not have common sense. Our elders of yesteryear used to call that kind of a person an educated fool. Schools, books, trainers, and your experiences can help you obtain knowledge, but wisdom according to James, comes from God. I also used to think that a person who had accumulated a significant amount of birthdays could be assured of the reality of possessing wisdom until I met my share of "old fools." James the brother of Jesus is rather candid when writing about wisdom and doesn't mince his words. You can't purchase it, you can't win it, stumble upon it, nor can you inherit it. You must ask the God of our salvation and he will liberally give it to you. Hallelujah to the Lamb!

Day 25

Pray for Unity

I appeal to you, brothers and sisters, in the name of our Lord Jesus Christ, that all of you agree with one another in what you say and that there be no divisions among you, but that you be perfectly united in mind and thought.
I Corinthians 1:10

Unity in the body of Christ can only come into fruition when all believers respect and follow the mandate of the Master. Jesus prayed for unity, the Spirit pleaded for unity, and the Father has presented a plan for unity in the word of God. We are charged by the apostles to emulate this model. The prophet Amos suggests that "If two walk together, both must agree… Amos 3:3. And David wrote, "Behold how good and pleasant it is for brethren to dwell together in unity." Our devotional today attempts to underscore the theme: pray for unity. First, we will notice the prayer of Jesus for unity among believers. In John 17; the Lord is observed pouring out His heart regarding the unity between Him and the Father. He clearly yearns and values unity with the body of Christ. The Lord desired a similar relationship with His disciples. If what Jesus prayed for was possible then; and experienced in the first-century church. And the prayer of Jesus becomes our prayer; why can't we experience the same unity in the 21st century church of Christ.

Let's not forget that we also must respond to the plea of the Holy Spirit for unity. The Spirit's plea for unity has not been answered in this generation. Men are still guilty of dividing the church. The church in America is certainly divided when you look at black and white Christians politically. It's the white evangelical church that won Trump the election. Unity must be the entire church's focus locally and globally. Let me be very candid, no one can claim to love the Lord, by accepting the Son of man; but, denying His plan for unity. To accept the person of Jesus Christ; requires, that we accept and follow God's plan. The church has been guilty of talking about unity but has failed to effectively implement the plan. In many cases, the Lord's church has not been a good example in maintaining the unity of the faith. Some churches have lost the desire for unity among its own membership; and with other congregations. We must make sure that our local congregations resist that spirit. We must rise above schisms, cliques, complacency, and carnality.

Day 26

Pray for Strength

*Fear not, for I am with you; be not dismayed, for I am
your God; I will strengthen you, I will help you, I will
uphold you with my righteous right hand.*
Isaiah 41:10

Years ago I use to hear Pastor Roosevelt Bradley of Gary Indiana, proclaim at the conclusion of his sermons, "Tough times don't last, but tough people do." I know what he means, because every time I've faced dark and tough times, God has toughened me up to be able to handle the task. No matter what we go through in life we as believers have been given the assurance that we can always bounce back. At the time of writing this meditation, it's October, the 10th month of the year. Technically, it's the fourth quarter of the year. You may have had a tough year but you still have time to turn it around. Fourth quarters are the time for comebacks, turnarounds, and come from behind wins for true winners. And if you are a believer you have already won, this scripture tells you so, it has a multi-prone message. The prophet Isaiah says because of God's presence, you don't have a reason to be afraid. Don't be disheartened, discouraged, or dispirited because I am your God says Jehovah. He then lists 3 key reasons as to why you should be content knowing that he is your God. As you read and meditate on this message, please find comfort in knowing that your prayers for strength is something that God is capable of delivering and he's committed to delivering.

Day 27

Pray for Increase of faith

*So then faith cometh by hearing, and hearing
by the word of God.
Romans 10:17*

If I told you that you could increase your faith by applying a simple principle would you be interested? When I was a musician years ago, we used to sing a song entitled "Lord Increase my Faith. The lyrics would say, Lord, increase my faith today. I want to go deeper and I want to go higher." If you really want to, incorporating a steady diet of the word of God in your life will make the difference. In the house that Margaret and I live in, when we first bought it, the motion sensor light in our yard would never come on. I soon found out that the only reason it wouldn't come on was because we never turned on the semi-concealed light switch. Once we located the switch and turned it on, we haven't had a problem since. The light comes on the moment someone walks within a certain proximity of the light and it turns off automatically after about one minute. That sort of reminds me how faith works.

The Bible is like the light switch; it turns on our faith. If you truly want your faith to increase and you want to accomplish some great things, getting in the word is the key to developing the caliber of faith to make it possible.

Dive into the word of God and learn about the character of God and about his plan of redemption for mankind. Study the character of Christ and be inspired by the Heroes of the faith in Hebrews chapter 11. You will be amazed at how God used misfits and ordinary people to do some extraordinary things.

Day 28

Pray for Growth of the Church

Praising God, and having favour with all the people. And the Lord added to the church daily such as should be saved.
Acts 2:47

During this 30 day consecration period, be sure to pray for your church's growth. We learn from the early church that God is the one who grows churches. When churches are strong in the area of the five purposes, they grow. This is always true. A healthy church grows when it's strong in evangelism, serving in ministry, vibrant in worship, authentic in fellowship and committed to discipleship. Your church will grow qualitatively or quantitatively. I was reading up on some church growth nuggets recently and the experts guarantee that three simple tips would grow your church instantaneously.

The first tip is work on your welcome. When a first-time guest visits your church, it should always be followed up with a note, an email or a phone call. When people join your church or frequently visit, learn their name, it makes them feel comfortable when they are no longer the new guy. Secondly, invest in young people. 35% of millennials don't attend service, resources must be invested in programming for that generation. It's important that they don't just watch worship, they must be a part of it. The last thing is increase your accessibility. It's a must to have live stream at your church, because the best and most loyal members just don't come to church every Sunday, but you must make it available. Make it easy to give too, via multiple online venues. Although we have prayed and will pray for God to add to the church, we must be willing to roll up our sleeves and work.

Day 29

Pray that your Pastor is Renewed and Refreshed

Obey your leaders and submit to them, for they are keeping watch over your souls, as those who will have to give an account. Let them do this with joy and not with groaning, for that would be of no advantage to you.
Hebrews 13:17

It is a blessing for a pastor to have a designated group of seasoned prayer warriors interceding on his behalf before the Lord. Having that type of covering is invaluable. On the other hand, as you grow in the word and in your faith you should see the necessity of praying for your own pastor. He or she has the burden of leadership that wears him or her down. I mentioned earlier how the local pastor is overworked, and I must admit they are also underpaid. That's why it's so important to pray that God renews him and refreshes him.

In the past years, far too many pastors suffered from burnout because they never took vacations or never invested in self-care. I remember years ago, I would go on vacation and would always end up flying back Saturday evening so that I would be at home to preach Sunday. I would also spend a significant amount of my vacation time in sermon preparation. That was grossly unfair to my wife and kids. While you pray for your pastor's renewal, please know that being renewed does more than keep him from burnout, it also allows him to be fresh. When He's fresh, sermons are "in time" messages and the vision of the church becomes easier to cast. This text in Hebrews reminds us how the pastor watches over the souls of his congregants and will one day have to give an account to God. So clearly it benefits you when you lighten the load of the pastor of the church. Lastly, you'd be surprised at how much it warms the heart of the pastor for him to know that you're praying for him or her. This simple act of prayer both encourages and reassures pastors. It reassures me, even though they may sometimes nod during my sermons, that they love my family, the church and me enough to do so.

Day 30

Pray for Financial Freedom and Prosperity

Give, and it shall be given unto you; good measure, pressed down, and shaken together, and running over, shall men give into your bosom. For with the same measure that ye mete withal it shall be measured to you again.
Luke 6:38

In one of the clearest examples of the law of the harvest principle in Scripture, Jesus tells us, "Give, and it will be given to you. They will pour into your lap a good measure—pressed down, shaken together, and running over. For by your standard of measure it will be measured to you in return, it's just a fact: you can never out give God. The Old Testament prophet Malachi certainly believed this principle. Through him, God instructed the people to bring Him the full tithe and said, "'Test Me now in this,' says the Lord of hosts, 'if I will not open for you the windows of heaven and pour out for you a blessing until it overflows'" (Mal. 3:10).

To 'tithe' is to give ten percent of our income. I started years ago living by the 10-10-80 plan. I pay 10 percent to myself by way of savings. I return 10 percent back to God, and usually, it's more, but that's the benchmark. I live on the rest, which is 80%. It takes a lot of self-control, but it's been paying off. I must confess there have been times that I mistakenly spent more than the desired 80 percent. Years ago, there were a few times I wasn't able to save the whole 10%, but I haven't missed a tithe in 30-plus years. For some strange reason, what I give to God, I never miss it. It's inexplicable. Free yourself from the bondage of being cheap with God and watch your life change exponentially.

About the Author

Pastor Ira J. Acree has pastored the Greater St. John Bible Church on Chicago's Westside for 29 years. He's a tireless advocate for empowerment, championing principles of entrepreneurship, education, economics and evangelism. He has a Bachelor of Arts in political science from the University of Illinois at Chicago, a Masters of Arts in Christian ministry from North Park Theological Seminary and a Doctorate of Ministry from Midwest Theological Institute. Most people know him from his social justice work within the Chicago's activist community. Although writing books, leading his congregation and spending time with his family keeps him very busy, Acree still has managed to stay at the forefront of justice on issues of local and national relevance for the last 18 years. He has two children, Marcus, 29 and Nicole, 26 and he's been married to the former Miss Margaret Hill for 30 years. He is the author of two books, *The Man In the Mirror* and *In Pursuit of Mr. Right*. Rev. Acree also hosts a weekly telecast on CAN-TV called "All Hands on Deck."

Direct comments or requests to:

> Pastor Ira J. Acree
> Greater St. John Bible Church
> 1256 N. Waller Ave
> Chicago, IL 60651
> (773) 378-3300

About the Publisher

Let us bring your story to life! With Life to Legacy, we offer the following publishing services: manuscript development, editing, transcription services, ghostwriting, cover design, copyright services, ISBN assignment, worldwide distribution, and eBook production and distribution.

Throughout the entire production process, you maintain control over your project. We also specialize in family history books, so you can leave a written legacy for your children, grandchildren, and others. You put your story in our hands, and we'll bring it to literary life! We have several publishing packages to meet all your publishing needs.

Call us at: 877-267-7477, or you can also send e-mail to: Life2Legacybooks@att.net. Please visit our Web site: www.Life2Legacy.com

www.ingramcontent.com/pod-product-compliance
Lightning Source LLC
Chambersburg PA
CBHW031657040426
42453CB00006B/331